T_o .. No.

F_{rom} Duncan........
& BECKY.
X X
Lots of Love

"So many things we love are
you, I can't seem to explain
except by little things, but
flowers and beautiful handmade t
hings - small stitches. So much
of our reading and thinking, so
many sweet customs and so much
of our...well, religion.
It is all <u>you</u>. I hadn't realized it
before. This is so vague but do you
see a little, dear Grandma? I want
to thank you."

ANNE MORROW LINDBERGH,
from "Bring Me A Unicorn"

"...grandmas need not indulge in
superhuman exploits to be remembered.
They are remembered for themselves,
endeared in the hearts of their
grandchildren from the first moments of
recognition, an instinctive love born of
that special relationship which is second
only to that enjoyed between a mother
and her child."

JACK HALLAM,
from "To Grandma with love"

I believe in grandmothers —
Tall ones, short ones, chubby and thin,
With big patch pockets for hiding things in.
I believe in grandmothers —
Older ones, younger ones, and in-between
Who say we're successful
When towels are clean!
I believe in grandmothers —
Who give us the moon and show us a star
By letting us know
We outshine them by far!

JUNE MASTERS BACHER

"*Dear old lady rich with our love
forever, heart of our home,
That's Grandmother.*"

URSULA O'LEARY, Age 11

"*Your Granny loves you. No matter
what you do.*"

PAUL MYERS, Age 10,
from "Grandmas & Grandpas"

"*When I fall and cut my knee she takes me in and laughs. I love her gentle loving touch, it makes me feel so safe.*"

KAREN WILSON, Age 10,
from "To the World's Best Grandma"

"*Grandma, you're always on my side. If you're not - I know I must be wrong.*"

MARCO FONDACARO

"[My grandmother] was the one member of my immediate family who most understood me, or so I thought at the time. Looking back, I think it was not so much her understanding as it was the sheer force of her encouragement that helped me through those years...."

LINDA SUNSHINE,
from "To Grandmother With Love"

"*The importance of grandparents in the life of little children is immeasurable. A young child with the good fortune to have grandparents nearby benefits in countless ways. It has a place to share its joys, its sorrows, to find a sympathetic and patient listener, to be loved.*

A child without grandparents can feel the lack of roots and a lack of connectedness. It misses a chance to link up with the past. Questions and answers about the 'old days' locate a child historically in his own small world. It provides a sense of inner security and a feeling of belonging."

EDWARD WAKIN

"*If God had intended us to follow recipes,
He wouldn't have given us
grandmothers.*"

LINDA HENLEY, b.1951

"*Some grans smell of lavender soap,
some grans smell of French perfume. My
gran smells of pastry and new bread and
peppermints. My gran smells gorgeous.*"

PETER

"*A faint aroma of gingerbread and all good things mixed together seems to linger all round a grandmother.*"

ELSPETH GORDON, Age 12

"*I loved their home. Everything smelled older, worn but safe; the food aroma had baked itself into the furniture.*"

SUSAN STRASBERG,
from "Bittersweet"

"*Because* [grandparents] *are usually
free to love and guide and befriend
the young without having to take
daily responsibility for them, they
can often reach out past pride and
fear of failure and close the space
between generations.*"

JIMMY CARTER, b.1924

"*H*er manner of storytelling evoked
tenderness and mystery as she put her face
close to mine and fixed me with her big,
believing eyes. Thus was the
strength that was developing in me
directly infused from her."

MAXIM GORKY (1868-1936)

"*Slow. Grandparents at Play.*"

ANONYMOUS
Traffic sign in Orange Harbor mobile-home park, Florida

"*A granny is jolly, and when she laughs, a warmness spreads over you.*"

J. HAWKSLEY, Age 11

"The hair on her head is silvery and her eyes sparkle with youth from behind an ageing skin. She is soft and tender, her love flows and blossoms, like a flower. She has distant memories that are treasured from within, and crystal clear. They do a great service and we would be nowhere without them. There is no replacement for a good thoroughbred Nan. I wouldn't be without mine."

MISS K. PARSONS, Age 17

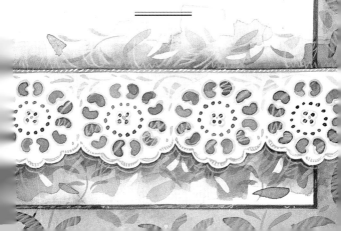

"*I* like to think that grandparents have a certain measure of invincibility. They get better with age, never worse. As the toy horse explained to the velveteen rabbit, 'Generally by the time you are real most of your hair has been loved off, your eyes drop out, and you get loose at the joints and very shabby. But these things don't matter at all, because once you are real you can't be ugly, except to people who don't understand.' Grandparents are indeed real. And are they ever ugly? Surely not, for the children do understand."

LANIE CARTER,
from "Congratulations! You're Going To Be a Grandmother"

*I*f nothing is going well, call your
grandfather or grandmother.

ITALIAN PROVERB

"*G*randma always made you feel she
had been waiting to see just you all day
and now the day was complete."

MARCY DeMAREE

"Thanks go to all grandmothers everywhere, for knowing what needs doing and doing it.
Whether it's a potty or a hug or a long walk or a bandage or a cup of tea.
Or doing the dishes."

PAM BROWN, b.1928

"*The history of our grandparents is*
remembered
not with rose petals
but in the laughter and tears of their
children
and their children's children.
It is into us
that the lives of grandparents have gone.
It is in us that their history
becomes a future.

CHARLES & ANN MORSE,
from "Let this be a day for grandparents"

"*The nice thing about her, is that she says that I've got two homes, my home and their home.*"

JULIA GAMBOLD, Age 9

"*In such a time of family mobility and changing family life-styles, a child needs to learn about his roots, and the grandparents are the roots.*"

LANIE CARTER,
from "Congratulations! You're Going To Be a Grandmother"

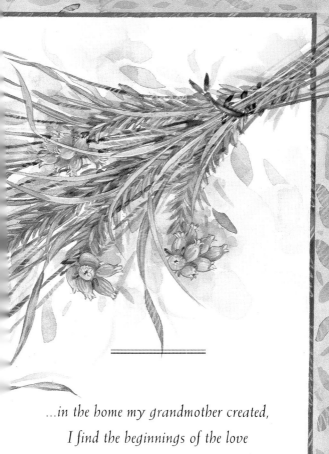

...in the home my grandmother created,

I find the beginnings of the love

I have inherited.

LOIS WYSE,
extract from "Inheritance"

"...grandmas need not indulge in
superhuman exploits to be remembered.
They are remembered for themselves,
endeared in the hearts of their
grandchildren from the first moments of
recognition, an instinctive love born of
that special relationship...."

JACK HALLAM